Compan......... .. ..

**THE MURDER AND MARTYRDOM
OF THE SALVADOREAN JESUITS**

Companions of Jesus

THE MURDER AND MARTYRDOM
OF THE SALVADOREAN JESUITS

Jon Sobrino SJ

First published 1990

Catholic Fund for Overseas Development (CAFOD)
2 Romero Close, Stockwell Road, London SW9 9TY, England

Catholic Institute for International Relations (CIIR)
22 Coleman Fields, London N1 7AF, England

Scottish Catholic International Aid Fund (SCIAF)
5 Oswald Street, Glasgow G1 4QR, Scotland

Trócaire-Irish Catholic Agency for World Development,
169 Booterstown Avenue, Blackrock, Co. Dublin, Ireland.

Translated from the unpublished manuscript, 'Compañeros de Jesus:
El asesinato-martirio de los jesuitas salvadoreños'.

ISBN 1 85287 066 4

Translated by Dinah Livingstone

Cover design by Jan Brown Designs

Printed in England by the Russell Press Ltd,
Bertrand Russell House, Gamble Street, Nottingham NG7 4ET

CONTENTS

Introduction

I have often been asked to write something immediately after some tragedy happened in El Salvador: the murder of Rutilio Grande, Archbishop Romero, the four North American women, to name only the most prominent cases. All these were occasions for both sorrow and indignation. But in some way or another we who survived managed to transform these feelings quite quickly into hope and service. In my case, this took the form, as we say, of analysing the events theologically. This time it was different. In order to write you need a clear head and courage in your heart, but in this case, for days my head was just empty and my heart frozen.

Now, some time later, as I am gradually feeling calmer, I am setting out to write these reflections. I do it in grateful homage — a small unnecessary homage perhaps — to my six martyred brothers. I am also doing it to try and bring some light and cheer to those of us who are still in this world, a cruel world which murders the poor and those who cast their lot with them, a world which also tries to paralyse those who are alive by killing their hope.

I am writing personally, because at the moment with my memory of my murdered brothers still fresh in my mind, I cannot do it any other way. Later on will be the time to interpret what happened in a more considered and analytical way, but now I couldn't do it. And I prefer to do it this way because perhaps writing like this under the impact of sorrow and my sense of loss I may be able to communicate a little of what hundreds of thousands of Salvadoreans have also felt. Between 70,000 and 75,000 people have died in El Salvador, but now that it has hit home to me, I

1

have felt something of the sorrow and indignation that so many Salvadoreans must have felt, peasants, workers, students, and especially mothers, wives, daughters when their loved ones were been killed.

First, I am going to relate simply what I felt when I heard the news and during those first days, in a very personal way. This experience is not important in itself, because it is only a drop in the ocean of tears that is El Salvador, but perhaps it may help to convey the pain of the Salvadorean people. After that I shall offer some general reflections on my friends and various important matters that their martyrdom raises. I shall speak of them as a group, especially the five who worked in the Central American University, the UCA, whom I knew best. I shall say a bit more about Ignacio Ellacuría because I lived with him for longer and it was he who most often put into words what these Jesuits accepted as fundamental in their lives and work.

1
'Something terrible has happened'

From November 13th I was in Hua Hin, about 200 kilometres from Bangkok in Thailand, giving a short course on christology. I was following the tragic events taking place in El Salvador on the radio and I had managed to speak to the Jesuits by telephone. They told me they were all well, and Ellacuría had just come back from Europe and entered the country with no problems. That same Monday 13th the Army had searched our house, room by room, and the Archbishop Romero Centre in the UCA, without further consequences.

Very late on the night of November 16th — it would have been eleven o'clock in the morning in San Salvador — an Irish priest woke me up. While half asleep, he had heard news on the BBC saying that something serious had happened to the UCA Jesuits in El Salvador. To reassure himself he had phoned London and then he woke me up. 'Something terrible has happened,' he told me. 'It is not very clear, but it seems they have murdered a Jesuit from the UCA, I don't know whether it is the Rector. London will give you more information.'

On the way to the telephone, I thought, although I did not want to believe it, that they had murdered Ignacio Ellacuría. Ellacuría, a brave and stubborn man, was not a demagogue but a genuine prophet in his writings, and ever more publicly on television. A little while ago an ordinary Salvadorean woman had said to me after seeing him on television: 'Not since they murdered Archbishop Romero has anyone spoken out so plainly in this country.' All these thoughts were going through my head on my short walk to the phone.

On the other end of the telephone in London was a great friend of mine and all the Jesuits in El Salvador, a man who has shown great solidarity with our country and our church. He began with these words: 'Something terrible has happened.' 'I know,' I replied, 'Ellacuría.' But I didn't know. He asked me if I was sitting down and had something to write with. I said I had and then he told me what had happened. 'They have murdered Ignacio Ellacuría.' I remained silent and did not write anything, because I had already been afraid of this. But my friend went on: 'They have murdered Segundo Montes, Ignacio Martín-Baró, Amando López, Juan Ramón Moreno and Joaquín López y López.' My friend read the names slowly and each of them reverberated like a hammer blow that I received in total helplessness. I was writing them down hoping that the list would end after each name. But after each name came another, on to the end. The whole community, my whole community, had been murdered. In addition, two women had been murdered with them. They were living in a little house at the entrance to the university and because they were afraid of the situation they asked the fathers if they could spend the night in our house because they felt safer there. They were also mercilessly killed. Their names are Julia Elba, who had been the Jesuits' cook for years, and her fifteen-year-old daughter Celina. As in the case of Rutilio Grande, when two peasants were murdered with him, this time two ordinary Salvadorean women died with the Jesuits.

Then my friend in London started giving me the details that were coming through in international telegrams. The killers were about thirty men dressed in military uniform. He told me they had taken three of the Jesuits out into the garden and tortured and machine-gunned them there. The other three and the two women they had machine-gunned in their beds. My friend could hardly go on speaking. Like many others during those days he had no words to express what had happened. He managed to give me a few words of comfort and solidarity and finally he wondered what strange providence had seen to it that I was not in our house at the time.

I spent several hours, or rather several days, unable to react. As I said at the beginning, on other tragic occasions we recovered our courage fairly quickly and were fired with a sense of service which made us active, in some way alleviating our sorrow by pushing the scenes of terror out of our heads. The masses we celebrated for the martyrs even filled us with joy. But this time, for me, it was different. The distance made me feel helpless and alone. And the six murdered Jesuits were my community, they were really my family. We had lived, worked, suffered and enjoyed ourselves together for many years. Now they were dead.

I do not think I have ever felt anything like it. I told the Irish priest who was with me that night that it was the most important thing that had happened to me in my whole life. I do not think that is an exaggeration. My long years in El Salvador, my work, including risks and conflicts, the difficult situations I had been through, even my religious life as a priest, seemed much less important things than the death of my brothers. They did not seem very real in comparison with these deaths. I felt a real breakdown in my life and an emptiness that nothing could fill. During those moments I remembered the biblical passage about the mothers of the murdered children who wept and could not be comforted. When I thought about things in my normal life, writing, talks and classes, the things I had been doing for the last sixteen years in El Salvador and might be doing in the future, it all seemed unreal to me with nothing to do with the reality. The most real reality — as I have often written from El Salvador — is the life and death of the poor. From thousands of miles away, and although I was still alive, the death of my brothers was a reality, compared to which everything else seemed little or nothing. Or rather, a reality which forced me to look at everything else from its standpoint. The Church, the Society of Jesus, faith, were not for me in those moments realities in terms of which — as it were, from a distance — I could understand or interpret their deaths, but the reverse. As a result of these deaths all those realities became questions for me and, very slowly — and I say this with gratitude — answers too to what is most fundamental in our lives: God, Jesus, vocation, the people of El Salvador.

I kept asking myself too why I was alive, and the Irish priest who was with me asked me the same question. I wanted to answer with the traditional words: 'I am not worthy.' But really there was no answer to that 'why?', and I didn't dwell on the question. Instead I began to have a feeling of irreparable loss. The UCA will never be the same, and I shall never be the same. After living and working with these brothers for so many years, it had become second nature to me to rely on them for my own life and work. Whatever idea, whatever plan came into my head, always ended the same way: 'but they're not there any more'. Ellacuría is not there any more to finish the book we were editing together. Juan

Ramón is no longer there to organise the January course on Archbishop Romero. Amando is no longer there to finish the next issue of the *Revista Latinoamericana de Teología*. Nacho is no longer there to give the psychology of religion course I'd asked him to give for the master's in theology. Montes is no longer there to understand the problems of the refugees and human rights. Lolo — that's what we called Fr Joaquín López y López — is no longer there: he was usually silent, but had a great feel for the thoughts and hopes of the poor people he worked with in the Fe y Alegría education programme. The examples I've given are not important in themselves, of course, but I give them to show that I had lost the direct links which connected me to real life. And I remembered from my years studying philosophy that a writer — I don't remember who — defined — I'm not sure if it was death or hell — as the total absence of relationships.

This was my experience in the first hours and days. It was my strongest sensation, beyond any doubt, but it wasn't the only one. The next morning the people on the course came up to me and embraced me in silence, many of them in tears. One of them told me that the death of my brothers was the best explanation and confirmation of the class we had held the previous day about Jesus, Yahweh's suffering servant, and the crucified people. The comment cheered me a little, not because it referred approvingly to my theology, of course, but because it linked my Jesuit brothers with Jesus and the oppressed. That same morning we had a mass in Hua Hin with an altar decked with flowers in the beautiful Asian style, with the name of El Salvador written on it and eight candles, which people from different Asian and African countries — who were acquainted with grief and death — lit in turn while I spoke the names of the eight victims. That night in another city five hours away by car, I had another mass with various Jesuits and many lay co-workers working with refugees from Vietnam, Burma, Cambodia, the Philippines, Korea... They also knew about suffering and could understand what had happened in El Salvador. On Saturday and Sunday back in Bangkok, I gave two talks — as I had been asked to give beforehand — on Jesus and the poor. Personally I did not feel much like speaking, but I thought I owed it to my brothers and talking about them was the best possible way of presenting the life and death of Jesus of Nazareth and his commitment to the poor today. Of course in Thailand, a country with a tiny number of Christians, someone asked me ingenuously

6

and incredulously: 'Are there really Catholics who murder priests in El Salvador?'

So it was not all darkness and being alone. I began to hear the reactions in many places, the solidarity of many Jesuits all over the world, the clear words of Archbishop Rivera, the promise by Fr Kolvenbach, our Father General, to come to El Salvador for Christmas, the immediate offer by various Jesuits from other countries to come to El Salvador and continue the work of those who had been murdered, the mass in the Gesu, the Jesuit Church in Rome, with about 600 priests at the altar, another mass in Munich with more than 6,000 students, masses in the US, Spain, England, Ireland and many more all over the world. I also received cards and telephone calls, full of tears and sorrow, but also full of love and gratitude to the six Jesuits. When they told me about the funeral mass in the Archbishop Romero chapel, with Jesuits determined to carry on the work of the UCA, little by little I came out of the dark and got my courage back. From what I can tell, the human and Christian reaction to this murder has been unique, only comparable perhaps to the reaction to Archbishop Romero's murder. Politically there is no doubt that this murder has had the most repercussions since Archbishop Romero's. In several countries, they tell me, nothing has so galvanised the Jesuits as these martyrs. If this has been so, we can say without triumphalism that this martyrdom has already begun to produce good, and this is what keeps up our hope now, even though our sorrow and sense of loss has not diminished.

I have described this experience because I want to say that now I understand a little better what this world's victims mean. The figures — 70,000 in El Salvador — are horrifying, but when these victims have particular names and are people who have been very close to you, the sorrow is terrible. I have told this story because I also wanted to say simply that I loved my murdered and martyred brothers very much. I am very grateful to them for what they gave me in their lives and for what they have given me in their death. Finally I have told the story so that what I am going on to say can be more easily understood. I am not going to say anything extraordinary but things that are well known. I do so honestly and sincerely, not as a matter of course but with the conviction aroused by this tragic event. First I am going to say a few words about who these Jesuits were and then I will reflect a little about important matters that their deaths have thrown light on.

2
Who were they?

Who were they? Many things could be said about them. When their biographies are written, some of them, like that of Ellacuría, the rector of the university, will fill several volumes, because his life of 59 years was prodigiously creative intellectually, in Church and religious matters and in politico-social analysis. Others, like Fr Lolo's, may be shorter, not because in his long life of 70 years he did not do many good things in the San José day school, his early years at the UCA and his last twenty years of direct service to the poor in Fe y Alegría,* but because his humble and simple temperament made him always want to be unnoticed. There will be such a lot to say about the others too. Segundo Montes was 56, a sociologist; he spent many years in the school and the UCA, he investigated the people's problems, especially refugees, he was the director of the UCA Institute of Human Rights. Nacho Martín-Baró was 47, academic vice-rector, a social psychologist who assiduously studied the problems of poor people, the psycho-social consequences of poverty and violence, religion as a force for liberation. Juan Ramón Moreno was 56, master of novices, professor of theology, vice-director of the Archbishop Romero Centre, which was, by the way, partially destroyed on the same day as the murders. Amando López, was 53, rector of the diocesan seminary of San Salvador, rector of the San José school and of the university of Managua during the Sandinista revolution, and professor of theology in the UCA. And as well as all these 'titles'

---

* A network of semi-vocational schools providing an education for the poor in marginalised rural and urban communities. Started in 1945 by a Venezuelan Jesuit, Fe y Alegría ('faith and joy') now operates some 350 such schools in twelve Latin American countries. In El Salvador it educates 20,000-40,000 young people.

we will have to mention all their devotion in their daily work of looking after the ordinary people who came to them with their problems, their Sunday pastoral work in parishes and poor suburban and rural communities, Santa Tecla, Jayaque, Quezaltepeque, Tierra Virgen, their struggles to build things in these poor places, a little clinic, a nursery, or put a tin roof over a few poles to create a church. We shall also need to write the biographies of Julia Elba and Celina, perhaps in just a few pages but telling the story of their lives as Salvadoreans and Christians, their poverty and suffering, daily struggle to survive, their hopes for justice and peace, their love for Archbishop Romero and faith in the God of the poor.

I cannot write their biographies here, but I should like to say a few words about what impressed me most in these Jesuits as a group — although of course there were differences between them. I want to suggest what is their most important legacy to us.

Before all else they were human beings, Salvadoreans, who tried to live honestly and responsibly in the midst of the tragedy and hope of El Salvador. This may not seem adequate praise for glorious martyrs, but it is where I want to start, because living in the midst of the situation of El Salvador, as in that of any part of the third world, is before all else a matter of humanity, a demand on all to respond with honesty to a dehumanising situation, which cries out for life and which is inherently an inescapable challenge to our own humanity.

These Jesuits, then, were human in a very Salvadorean way, solid, not like reeds to be swayed by any wind. They worked from dawn to dusk and now will have presented themselves before God with their calloused hands, maybe not from physical work, but certainly from work of all sorts: classes, writing, the important if monotonous work of administration, masses, retreats, talks, interviews, journeys and lectures abroad. Sometimes they gave brilliant performances, as participants in international congresses or appearing on television, in discussion with well-known personalities, diplomats and ambassadors, bishops, political and trade union leaders, intellectuals, receiving international awards. On 1 November Segundo Montes received a prize in the United States Congress for his investigations into refugees, and Ellacuría, a few days before he returned to El Salvador, received from the mayor of Barcelona an important prize awarded to the UCA. They worked sometimes in the parishes, in the communities and in their offices, talking to the simple people, to peasants and

10

refugees, to mothers of the disappeared, trying to solve the everyday problems of the poor. Sometimes — most of their time — they followed the dull routine of the calendar — even though in El Salvador no day is like another, — working at everyday tasks, meeting the demands of that structure of reality called 'time'. Through this everyday work they accumulated a great knowledge of the country and the credibility which came from being always at their posts; this gave them great prestige and massively reinforced their work and influence.

They were men of spirit, although outwardly they were not 'spiritual' in the conventional sense. From Ellacuría I learnt the expression 'poor with spirit', to express adequately the relationship between poverty and spirituality. Above all I want to call these Jesuits 'men with spirit'. And this spirit showed itself, as St Ignatius recommends in the meditation to attain love, 'more in deeds than in words'.

Above all, a spirit of service. If anything emerges clearly from this community, it is their work, to the point where they called us fanatics. But it was work that was really service. In this they were certainly outstanding disciples of St Ignatius. They did not think of work as a way of pursuing a career. Some of them could easily have been world figures in their professions, and some indeed were, although they never directly sought to be. It was not that they did not enjoy peace and quiet. But given the needs of the country and Ellacuría's creativity in always proposing new plans and never letting us rest on our laurels, work is what dominated the community. This had its disadvantages but above all it was the witness of lives dedicated to serving others. They nearly all did pastoral work in poor parishes and communities on Sundays after an exhausting week and on many Saturday and Sunday afternoons they could be seen working in their offices. I remember, for example, that at times we discussed finishing the week's work in the UCA on Friday afternoons, and not at noon on Saturday, as was our practice, but the discussion always ended with these words: 'That's for the first world. In a poor country like ours, we have to work harder, not less hard.' In fact even the notion of holidays, never mind a sabbatical year, disappeared from our lives. And although this really excessive workload also had its dehumanising aspect and effects on health, these men lived this way because they were trying to respond to the countless urgent needs of the situation in El Salvador. I remember when Fr Kolvenbach visited us El Salvador Jesuits in 1988 — a very encouraging visit for which we are sincerely grateful — he recommended, as it was his responsibility to do, that we should not work to excess and that we should take care of our health and strength. And I remember that someone in the community replied that in situations like ours it is necessary to be indifferent to health or sickness, a short life or long, as St Ignatius says in the Principle and Foundation. It was not that we did not understand and were not grateful for what Fr Kolvenbach was telling us, but we wanted to stress that the situation in El Salvador — not just ascetic or mystical inclinations — required that we should be indifferent and available to give our lives and health. Whether or not this was exaggerated, these men saw their work as a way of serving and responding to the situation in El Salvador.

However, this work had a very particular aim: to serve the poor. When we used religious language, we spoke of the poor, those to whom God gives priority. When we used the language of Salvadorean history, we spoke of the mass of ordinary people. Really these are the same. We wanted to serve the millions of men and women who live lives unfit for human beings and sons and daughters of God. The deepest thing in these Jesuits' lives was this service and they really did have a spirit of compassion and pity. If they worked like fanatics and ran very conscious risks, it was because they had a gut reaction — like the good Samaritan, Jesus and the heavenly Father — when they saw a whole suffering people on the road. They never passed by on the other side like the priest and the Levite in the parable, so as to avoid meeting and being affected by the people's suffering. They never said no to anything people asked them if it was possible for them to oblige. They never sought refuge in academic work to avoid the needs of the people, as if university knowledge was not also subject to the primary ethical and practical requirement to respond to the cry of the masses. So the inspiration of all their work and service was this compassion and pity which they truly put first and last. The language they used as university men was of 'justice', 'transformation of structures', 'liberation', including, properly understood, 'revolution', but this was not a cold academic language, of ideology or politics. Behind it lay the real language of love for the Salvadorean people, the language of pity. With this people and for this people they lived many years. And they all made this people their own, although all of them except Father Lolo had been born in Spain. 'Your people shall be my people,' as Scripture says.

Their spirit was one of courage. They had energy and endurance for everything, for the constant hard work, for dealing with the thousand and one problems that arose every day in the university, strictly university problems and problems which arose day after day in the country and reached the university. So they had to combine classes with giving urgent help to some refugee or someone who had disappeared, they endlessly had to interrupt their writing to deal with calls and visits. There was not much external peace for working and sometimes it seemed that their shoulders were not broad enough to bear everything loaded on to them. But they did not withdraw from problems or let people down.

They had courage to keep going amid conflicts and persecutions. In the last fifteen years they received many threats from phone calls or anonymous letters, and especially in the newspapers with fantastic accusations in editorials and advertisements — sometimes paid for by the Army — which suggested in one way or another or plainly demanded the expulsion or annihilation of these Jesuits. In recent months clear threats appeared in the press and on television, especially against Ellacuría and Segundo Montes. The final threats were on the radio, when from the 12th November onwards all the transmitters were in government hands and issuing threats against the Jesuits and the Archbishop.

And as well as verbal threats, they suffered physical attacks. From 6th January 1976 — I remember the date very well — when they placed the first bomb in our university, there have been fifteen occasions when bombs have been planted, in the printroom, the computer centre, the library, the administration building. The last one exploded on 22nd July this year, partially destroying the printing press. The police came to our own house four times and on the last occasion they stayed for eleven hours. In February 1980 the house was heavily machine-gunned at night, and in October of the same year it was dynamited twice: on the 24th and three days later on the 27th. In 1983 a new bomb exploded in our house; this time because we had defended dialogue as the most human and Christian solution for the country. A tragic irony, but in those days the very word 'dialogue' was synonymous with betrayal.

So their service to the mass of the people was very aware of the risks. They accepted the risk perfectly naturally without any fuss, and not even through any special spiritual discernment, because one only discerns what is not clear and for these men it was

13

absolutely clear that they had to go on with their work in the country. That is why they remained in El Salvador and I never heard them saying they should leave, whatever the threats and dangers. Perhaps the very fact of their remaining in the country was a great service to many people who might have left if they had abandoned the country. In 1977, after Rutilio Grande was murdered, we all received death threats. The names of various UCA Jesuits were always on the lists of dangerous persons. And remember that in El Salvador leaflets were even thrown in the street saying 'Be a patriot, kill a priest'. Sometimes we spent nights in nuns' houses or with friendly families, but next day we all returned to work at the UCA. Only once, in November 1980, did Ellacuría leave the country under the protection of the Spanish embassy, because his name was top of a secret list of persons who were going to be killed. And remember that that year the threats were very real; it was the year in which Archbishop Romero was murdered, as were four priests, four North American women missionaries, a seminarian, the rector of the National University, the five principal leaders of the Democratic Revolutionary Front (FDR), and as always, hundred of peasants, workers, trade unionists, students, teachers, doctors, journalists... Ellacuría later returned to the country with no guarantee, fully aware that he was taking on all these risks again. There is no doubt that they were brave men, of a piece with the Salvadorean people who moulded them and who have given an example to the world of how to bear endless misfortunes, how to survive and how to struggle for life with a creativity that astonishes all those who know them. So these men were true Salvadoreans, and I should like to add that the courage, and honesty and service with which they lived was returned in full measure by this people. The people's sufferings transformed and purified them, by their hope they lived, and their love won their hearts for ever.

These men were also believers, Christians. I do not mention this here as something obvious or to be taken for granted, but as something central in their lives, something that really ruled all their lives. They were not 'pious' in the conventional sense, repeating 'Lord, Lord,' in the temple, but they were people who went out into the street to do God's will. So, when we spoke about matters of faith in the community, our words were sparing but really meant. We spoke about God's kingdom and the God of the kingdom, of Christian life as a following of Jesus, the historical Jesus, Jesus of Nazareth, because there is no other. In the

14

university — in teaching and theological writings, of course — but also in solemn moments and public acts we recalled our Christian inspiration as something central, as what gave life, direction, force and meaning to all our work, and explained the risks the university very consciously incurred. There was plain speaking about God's kingdom and the option for the poor, sin and the following of Jesus. This Christian inspiration of the university was never just rhetoric when these Jesuits talked about it, and people understood that this was really the university's inspiration. Even some who would have been reluctant to call themselves believers realised and were grateful because the Christian faith lived in this way made the university more Salvadorean.

It is difficult or impossible to see to the bottom of these men's hearts, their faith, but for me there is no doubt that they were great believers and that their lives only had meaning as followers of Jesus. What was their faith like? Thinking of each one of them singly, with their different life stories and characters, I feel fascinated and grateful above all for the fact that they did have great faith, because in countries like El Salvador faith is not something obvious, in the midst of so much injustice and so much silence from God, and I never fail to be impressed by the very fact that there is faith.

I think they believed in a God of life, who favours the poor, a beneficent utopia in the midst of our history, a God who gives meaning and salvation to our lives and hence a radical hope. I think they found God hidden in the suffering face of the poor and they found him crucified in the crucified people. And they also found God in those acts of resurrection, great and small, by the poor. And in this God-in-little — God ever littler — they found the God who is ever greater, the true inexhaustible mystery which impelled them along untrodden ways and to ask what had to be done. I should like to say of them what I have written elsewhere about Jesus of Nazareth. For them God was a good father, history's beneficent utopia, that attracted them and made them give more and more of themselves. In him they could rest and find the ultimate meaning of their lives. But for them the Father went on being God, the mystery beyond our control, and therefore he did not let them rest and drove them to keep seeking new things to do to respond to his new and sovereign will.

I have already said that our community was not very prone to put things into words, preferring to say them with our lives. Now my brothers have said them with their blood. But I want to mention someone they often did talk about: Archbishop Romero. And when they did they spoke the language of faith. Loving and admiring Archbishop Romero is not at all difficult, except for those who deny the light and have hearts of stone. But trying to follow him and accept all of Archbishop Romero is a matter of faith. I believe that for them, for me and so many others, Archbishop Romero was a Christ for our time and, like Christ, a sacrament of God. To come into contact with Archbishop Romero was like coming into contact with God. Meeting Archbishop Romero in person was like meeting God. Trying to follow Archbishop Romero was like following Jesus today in El Salvador. This is what my brothers wanted to do. I do not think that either the Lord Jesus or the heavenly Father are jealous of my speaking like this about Archbishop Romero. After all, Romero was God's most precious gift to us all in these times. And when you feel strongly attracted by a witness like Archbishop Romero, whom we have seen, heard and touched, I believe that it can truly be said that you are being attracted by Jesus and his gospel, the Jesus we have only read about and not seen definitively.

In any case if it is true that we all feel our faith supported by the faith of others, I have no doubt that our community was supported by the faith of others, by our brother Rutilio Grande, so many Salvadorean believers who proved their faith by shedding their blood, and by the faith of Archbishop Romero. I don't know whether I am projecting on to others what faith in God means for me, but I believe and hope that it is not just a projection. If I have learnt anything in El Salvador it is that faith is on the one hand something that cannot be delegated, like Abraham's when he stood alone before God, but on the other hand a faith supported by others. The two things combine in El Salvador, reinforcing each other. Thus amid so much darkness it continues to be possible, I believe, to have the light of faith. As the prophet Micah says, in a passage I have often quoted, it remains very clear that God requires us human beings to 'act justly and love tenderly' (cf Mic 6.8). And it is also clear — now in the bright darkness of the mystery — that thus we 'walk humbly with God' in history. The first thing, the absolute requirement of justice, is what clearly revealed to these Jesuits the real situation of the poor and — in their doing justice — made them resemble God. And the second, the difficult task of walking with God in this history of darkness — where can we get the strength to do it? I think what made it possible for them was the memory of Jesus, of his witnesses today

16

and the faith of the poor themselves. These brothers joined the current of hope and love which is still running through history in spite of everything, that historical current driven ultimately by the poor. They worked to make this utopian hope constantly increase and gain more body. but this hope also sustained them in their hope and faith. I believe they saw the poor from God's point of view and walked with them towards God. This, I believe, was what my brothers' faith was like.

These men, these believers, were lastly Jesuits. I believe they were profoundly 'Ignatian', although they sometimes did not appear very 'Jesuit', if I make myself clear, to those who are always waiting for the latest word from Rome or those who think that the Society is the most important thing that exists on the face of the earth. Nevertheless they were sincerely proud of being Jesuits. It is not that they were outstanding in everything Ignatian but they were outstanding in the essentials of the *Spiritual Exercises*. I remember that in 1974 Ellacuría and I gave a course on the *Exercises* from the Latin American viewpoint. And in 1983 in our Provincial Congregation we wrote a joint paper based on the structure of the *Exercises* to be presented to the General Congregation of that year. Normally it was left to us two and Juan Ramón Moreno to put into words what was Ignatian in our lives and work, but I believe the rest of them accepted and heartily shared this vision.

From St Ignatius we used to recall the great moments in the *Exercises*. The contemplation of the incarnation, to enable us to see the real world with God's own eyes, that is, a world of perdition, and to react with God's own compassion, that is, 'to make redemption'. And it is important to remember this because, as for many other Salvadoreans, it was not anger — which was sometimes completely justified — or revenge, much less hatred that was the motive force in their lives, but love: 'making redemption', as St Ignatius called it. We also used to stress Jesus' mission in the service of God's kingdom and translate this into our own historical situation: the meditation on the two standards with the inevitable alternatives of wealth and poverty, with the Ignatian intuition that poverty, accepted in a Christian way, leads to all good, whereas wealth, by its very nature, leads to all evil; taking on the sin of the world and the concealment of Christ's divinity in the passion, as St Ignatius says. Something that was very original and extremely relevant to our situation was Ignacio Ellacuría's interpretation of the meditation on our sins in the presence of the

17

crucified Christ. He related it to our third world, and asked what we have done to cause all these people to be crucified, what we are doing about their crosses and what we are going to do to bring them down from the cross. From him too I learnt to apply the expression 'crucified people' to our people. We should not only speak of Moltmann's 'crucified God', Ellacuría used to say, although this is necessary. He compared these people with Yahweh's suffering servant, as Archbishop Romero also intuitively did: the suffering servant is Jesus and the suffering servant is the crucified people. Our answer to these questions expressed with utter seriousness the conversion demanded by St Ignatius.

We also reinterpreted St Ignatius' ideal of 'contemplatives in action' as 'contemplatives in action for justice'. I do not know how much contemplation there was in their lives, in the conventional sense, but I have no doubt that their way of contemplating God's face in the world was in their action to change his face, hidden and disfigured in the poor and oppressed, into the face of the living God who gives life and raises from the dead.

These were the Ignatian ideals that moved this group. They put them into practice, with limitations of course, but I have no doubt it was these ideals that inspired them and they bore outstanding witness to them. And this spirit of St Ignatius is what gives us the clue to understanding how they saw themselves as Jesuits in the world today. They and Jesuits like them are the ones who are bringing about the changes that have taken place in the Society's mission to the world, a change comparable to Vatican II or Medellín and therefore a real miracle and gift of God. The Society's present mission was formulated as 'service of faith and promotion of justice' (32nd General Congregation, 1975), taking the form of an 'option for the poor' (33rd General Congregation, 1983). This change has been very radical. For the Society it has entailed conversion, abandoning many things and many ways of behaving, losing friendships with the powerful and their benefits and gaining the affection of the poor. It has meant above all returning to Jesus' gospel, to the Jesus of the gospel and to the poor for whom Jesus preached and was gospel, that is, good news. But it has also been a very important change and very beneficial, especially for third world countries. It has meant that the Society has become truly Christian and truly Central American. It has meant keeping the Society's identity in a way that makes it relevant to our world and giving it a relevance that helps it to rediscover its

Ignatian identity. This is no small benefit to the Society, and was produced very largely by Jesuits like the six who were murdered.

Jesuits like them have proved the truth of something else our 33rd General Congregation said: 'We cannot carry out our mission of service to the faith and the promotion of justice without paying a price.' In the last fourteen years since these words were said, many Jesuits have been threatened, persecuted and imprisoned in the third world. I believe the number of Jesuits murdered is about twenty, seven of them in El Salvador, Fr Rutilio Grande and now the six from the UCA. Although it is tragic, it needs repeating: these crosses are what show that the choice made by the Society was correct, Christian and relevant to the needs of today. These crosses also show above all that this choice has been put into practice. And again this is no small benefit their martyrdom has given the Society.

I believe, therefore, that they were Ignatians and Jesuits of the sort the Society wants today. Without fuss, sugary words or triumphalism they felt themselves to be Jesuits, again more in deed than word. Certainly it was they who asked Ignatius' two great questions: 'Where am I going, why am I going?' They tried to answer these questions honestly, without dressing them up in florid devotional language or disguising them in diplomatic worldly caution. They did not even cover them with discerning insights that can sometimes be paralysing, because, as I said before, the obvious is not an object of discernment. They were people who sought the greater glory of God and remembered Ignatius' saying: 'The more universal the good is, the more it is divine.' This is how they saw their work, especially their university work, which was directed towards the transformation of the structures of their country, so that salvation could reach more people. They were in the vanguard, in the trenches, fighting for solutions to the gravest problems of our time. They were the ones closest to the noise of battle. If they fell in the battle, it is because they were in it.

This is how I remember them, as human beings who were honest about reality, as believers in God and followers of Jesus, and as leading late twentieth-century Jesuits in a Third World country. Of course they had limitations and defects, both singly and as a group. They were sometimes harsh and stubborn , even pig-headed, though not to defend what was theirs but in fighting for what they considered better for the country, the Church and the Society. But this did not prevent them living and working in unity, bearing each other's burdens, and supported by each other's spirit.

19

In this way they were companions of Jesus and they fulfilled the mission of the Society of Jesus, the Jesuits, in the world today.

3

Why were they killed?

Why were they killed? Now I want to try to throw a little light on their murder and martyrdom. A murder is darkness, but *sub specie contrarii* it throws light on many things. A martyrdom has its own strong light which says more than a thousand words about life and faith. So I am offering these reflections in search of light for us who are still alive, to clarify the reality in which we live and give us courage to transform it.

The answer to the question why were they killed goes on being extremely important because understanding who these Jesuits were and what they did depends on it. But not just this. The answer also enables us to understand what is going on in El Salvador and understand our faith, which, let us not forget, begins at the feet of a crucified figure who was executed by the powerful of this world. 'They kill those who get in their way,' Archbishop Romero used to say. And really these Jesuits did get in the way. There is no other explanation for all the verbal and physical attacks I mentioned earlier.

And who did they get in the way of? Who did they annoy? Their enemies and murderers used to accuse them of many things. They accused them of being communists and marxists; sometimes they said they were anti-patriotic; sometimes they even called them atheists. They even attacked them for being 'liberationists'. What an ironical and tragic distortion to use a term that is central to the gospel — 'liberation' — to denigrate a believer. In fact they did not mean anything in particular by these accusations, they were merely expressing their total repulsion and fervent wish to see them silenced, expelled from the country, disappeared or dead.

And remember that in this country even Paul VI was accused of being a 'communist' when he published *Populorum Progressio.*

Others made more specific accusations: They support the FMLN, they are its ideological 'front', they are responsible for the violence and war, etc. This assumes, of course, that the FMLN is the worst of evils in the country and anyone who supports them is automatically a murderer. Of course for the extreme right anyone is an FMLN 'front' who defends the poor and tells the truth about the violation of human rights: from trade unionists who are fighting for their rights and the committees of mothers of the murdered and disappeared, to the excellent *internacionalistas*, men and women who have left behind the peace and comfort of their own countries to serve the poor in El Salvador — even to Archbishop Rivera and Bishop Rosa Chávez and the Archdiocesan Legal Aid Office.

The first accusation is simply false. These Jesuits were honest human beings and Christian believers, convinced that Jesus brought a demand for liberation and the way to achieve it, total utopian liberation. Of course they were familiar with marxism, its useful contribution to the analysis of the oppression in the third world, and its serious limitations. But marxism was in no way their principal source of academic inspiration — Ellacuría was an eminent and creative disciple of the Spanish philosopher Zubiri. Neither was it their ultimate ideology for transforming society, much less what inspired their personal lives. That was the gospel of Jesus and from its standpoint they sought the best available scientific knowledge with which to scrutinise various ideologies and use them in the service of the poor.

The second accusation is not true either. This needs explaining in some detail so that the truth may be known about what happened. This is also to prevent people saying — or whispering, because hardly anyone dares at the moment to say it out loud — that even though it was tragic, they did seek their own death. (Things like this have been said in the past few years, even by prelates, when a priest has been killed.) However simple it may sound, what these Jesuits firmly supported and were really committed to was the mass of ordinary people, and nothing else. They repeated endlessly that it was not their role to support a political party or a particular government or even a particular popular movement. Their task was to judge them and support anything in them which helped bring justice to the people. In this too they were faithful to the words and spirit of Archbishop

Romero: 'Political processes must be judged according to whether they are or are not for the good of the people'. Therefore they analysed and supported what was positive and just in the popular movements, including the FMLN, but they criticised what they thought was politically mistaken, especially purely militarist tendencies abandoning the social and popular dimension, and what was morally reprehensible, especially a few acts of terrorism and murders of civilians by the FMLN. No one who has read the UCA's publications can be in any doubt about this.

Regarding the conflict and the war, I remember well that even in February 1981, after the FMLN's first major offensive, which failed, Ellacuría said then that the solution for the country lay in negotiation, words which the right regarded as treacherous and were not very agreeable to the left either. That same year, in the month of May, the journal ECA devoted a wholoe issue to dialogue and negotiation. Although they were not absolute pacifists, any more than Archbishop Romero was, although they understood and analysed the causes of the war, its tragic inevitability and possible legitimacy at the end of the seventies, they were not advocates of war: they regarded war as a terrible evil that ought to disappear. They were fully aware of the good things the FMLN has brought to the country and scandalised the extreme right by acknowledging them. They were fully aware of the creativity, heroism and love of many FMLN combatants. But this did not blind them to the evils of war, and they were never carried away in theory — or of course in practice — by what Archbishop Romero condemned as the mysticism of violence. With great human and ethical compassion, Ellacuría said plainly: 'The way of war has now given all it had to give; now we must seek the way of peace.'

Therefore they strongly supported dialogue and negotiation, especially in recent months. The university did everything it could to enable dialogue to take place by itself speaking to both sides. President Cristiani knows this perfectly well. Some of the Jesuits spoke to him a few times in private and the UCA invited him to be present on 19th September 1989 when it conferred an honorary doctorate on the president of Costa Rica, Oscar Arias, for his work for peace. In order to make dialogue easier they spoke to FMLN leaders, with some members of the government, all kinds of politicians and diplomats, including some military officers, but they did all this with the single purpose of supporting a more human and more Christian negotiated solution to the conflict. So they had knowledge, contacts, support for the positive and criticism of the negative things in the FMLN. There were also talks with some government forces, including support for anything that offered a little light in El Salvador's gloom and despair, whether this came from the government, political parties or the North American embassy, although obviously they remained firm in their denunciation of the abuses and violations of human rights committed by the army and the death squads, in stating the government's responsibility for these and denouncing unpunished crimes and the useless state of the administration of justice. They continued to unmask the dependency on the US. So they were not a 'front' for the FMLN, or of any other group or political project, although they analysed them all and promoted the good, whether it was much or little, that they found in them. If they were a 'front' for anyone, these Jesuits were a 'front' for the mass of ordinary people, the poor and oppressed in the country. And — this is the tragedy — it was for this that they were finally killed.

These things are well known in El Salvador. I have recalled them here in order to stress that none of the things they were accused of was the reason for their deaths. As in the case of Archbishop Romero, many other martyrs and Jesus of Nazareth, the simpler and deeper reason lay elsewhere. I mean that those who killed them gave false reasons, if it is possible to speak of 'reasons' for such an abominable crime. And of course these 'reasons' had no ethical justification. But fundamentally they did not make a mistake, just as , in spite of what Bultmann says, the execution of Jesus of Nazareth was not a mistake. There were no just reasons for eliminating them, but there was a necessity to eliminate them. And this necessity — tragically — is structural and does not derive from the cruelty of this or that person or group. It is the necessary reaction of the idols of death towards anyone who dares to touch them.

There is a deep conviction in Latin America that idols exist in this world. Puebla spoke of them and also Archbishop Romero in his last pastoral letter of 1979, certainly written with the help of Ellacuría. Liberation theology has done what is not done elsewhere and developed a theory of idols. As has been said so many times, but needs repeating because it continues to be a horrific reality, idols are historical realities, which really exist, which pass for divinities and reveal themselves with the characteristics of divinity. They claim to be ultimate reality, self-justifying, untouchable, offering salvation to their worshippers

24

even though they dehumanise them. Above all, they require victims in order to maintain their power. These idols of death were identified in El Salvador by Archbishop Romero as the idol of wealth, making capital an absolute — the first and most serious of idols and the originator of all the others — and the doctrine of national security. Then he added a serious warning to the popular organisations that they should not become idols themselves and never adopt a mystique of violence, even when violence became legitimate. So idols exist, and as Archbishop Romero chillingly said, you cannot touch them without being punished. 'Woe to anyone who touches wealth. It is like a high tension cable that burns you.' This is what happened to the six Jesuits and so many others.

The UCA Jesuits touched the idol by *telling the truth about the situation*, analysing its causes and putting forward the best possible solutions. But this activity, which would seem to be so good, so helpful, which ought to be praised and supported by all, is persecuted by the idols. The really terrible thing the Jesuits did was to tell the truth about El Salvador in their publications and public statements. They said that the most serious aspect was the massive, cruel and unjust poverty of the mass of the people. They said that when these masses, with every right and justice, organise simply in order to survive, they are repressed. All this continues to be true in El Salvador, although both Salvadorean and US government policies refuse to recognise it. These policies do not address this fundamental reality or seek a solution for it.

As well as making this fundamental prophetic declaration, they analysed the situation and its causes in a way appropriate to a university. In 1971 the UCA published a book on a famous teachers' strike which supported the teachers' case. Even then this cost them their government grant. They began to demand agrarian reform as the most radical and necessary solution to the country's ills. From then onwards their enemies realised that they were interfering with the idol. In 1972 the UCA published another important book revealing, denouncing and analysing the electoral fraud in the presidential elections. This fraud made people begin to lose faith permanently in a solution to the injustice coming from elections alone. In 1976, another important moment, when President Molina went back on the incipient (and minimal) agrarian reform, Ignacio Ellacuría published an editorial in the journal ECA entitled 'At your service, capital!' From then on they continued to tell the truth and objectively analyse the Salvadorean situation. They told the truth about poverty, unemployment, the horrific homelessness, lack of education and health, the truth about repression and violation of human rights, the truth about the progress of the war, about dependence on the US, and also the truth about the FMLN and the popular movements, their correct and mistaken actions and strategies... And so many other truths. As another expression of this desire for the truth, two years ago the UCA opened an institute of public opinion, directed by Fr Martín-Baró, which very soon became the most objective source of information about what Salvadoreans were thinking.

The truth, expressed in a university way, is what these Jesuits tried to tell and analyse as objectively as possible. This was acknowledged by countless international institutions, many politicians, ambassadors, analysts and journalists, who poured through the UCA to hear the truth about El Salvador from these men's own mouths. These visitors did not always agree with all their analyses, but everybody, with the exception of the extreme right, recognised their desire for the truth. So they were not spokesmen of any group or institution, they were spokesmen for the reality itself. If they had or recognised any bias, it was that they saw reality from the viewpoint of the poor. And if they told the truth so decidedly, it was because they were convinced that truth at least is on the side of the poor, and sometimes that is all they have on their side.

Telling the truth, communicating it in a way appropriate to a university, as these Jesuits did, or in a pastoral way, as Archbishop Romero did, has always been dangerous because the idols seek to hide their true face of death and necessarily generate lies in order to conceal themselves. Sin always seeks to hide itself, scandal to cover itself up. So telling the truth becomes an unmasking of lies, and that is not forgiven. The sin of the world, the structural injustice which brings death, is not only unjust but also tries to hide its evil nature, even pretending to be good. It may dress up as something desirable; it disguises reality by using euphemisms; 'freedom of expression,' 'democracy', 'elections', 'defence of the democratic and Christian Western world'. And the world of injustice and power which brings death to the poor creates a gigantic cover-up to conceal the scandal of the victims it produces, a cover-up compared with which Watergate or Irangate are small faults or venial sins.

So telling the truth does not just mean dissipating ignorance but fighting lies. This is essential work for a university and central to our faith. If I have learnt anything during these years in El Salvador it is that the world in which we live is simultaneously a world of death and a world of lies. And I discovered this in scripture. As Paul says, the world imprisons the truth with injustice. These Jesuits wanted to free the truth from the slavery imposed on it by the oppressors, cast light on lies, bring justice in the midst of oppression, hope in the midst of discouragement, love in the midst of indifference, repression and hatred. That is why they were killed.

The truth they told was lit by the knowledge produced in the university, as rationally and objectively as possible. But it was also and essentially lit by the poor. They accepted the prophet Isaiah's scandalous statement: the crucified people, disfigured and faceless, Yahweh's suffering servant has been placed by God as a light to the nations. This is, for those who seek the truth, the option for the poor. This option is not just a professional option, required by the Church and the Society of Jesus only of those who do pastoral work. It is a total option which affects every believer and all of us in what we know, hope, do and celebrate. It is a total option for the Church and for the university. This was the option these Jesuits made, in their academic work as in everything else. They believed — and experience confirmed it — that more can be seen from below than above, that reality can be known better from the standpoint of suffering and powerlessness of the poor, than from that of the powerful. So their truth was made possible by the poor.

However, the option also means returning to the poor the truth which is theirs, and so they returned to the poor the truth the university generated, to defend, enlighten and encourage them. The UCA made an option for the poor and put it into practice in various ways. In teaching they tried above all to communicate what the real national situation is — this is the major teaching material, the compulsory part of all courses. They wanted to give a voice to the reality of the lives of the vast majority of ordinary people — the true national reality and not the exceptions and anecdotes about it that are sometimes taught in universities — with its suffering, and also with its hope and creativity.

The question that dominated any research was to discover the reality of oppression and its causes in depth, and actively to offer the best solutions. This was a great ideal, difficult to attain, but one to which these Jesuits devoted immense effort. They tried to offer models, with real possibilities, of an economy, a policy, a technology for housing, education, health, an educational, artistic and cultural creativity, a Christian and liberating religion which would make life possible for ten million human beings at the end of this century in this small poor country of El Salvador. That was the goal of their research.

In its outreach the UCA opened itself directly and immediately to the mass of the people, through its publications, the numerous, brave and public stands it took, through the Institute of Human Rights, directed by Fr Montes, through the Information Centre and through the Archbishop Romero Centre in theological, pastoral and religious matters. They wanted to help generate a collective awareness in the country, which would be both critical and constructive and help the poor. Towards the popular movements these Jesuits were very open and strongly supported them insofar as they were the people, although not for their particular organisational line. Theoretically and practically they sought to explain the necessity, justice, identity and purpose of the popular movements. And this was strikingly visible in the university campus itself, which never closed its doors to trade unionists, the marginalised, the mothers of the disappeared, human rights groups, popular pastoral workers etc.

Truth told, analysed and presented in a university and Christian way, this is a kind of university that the idols will not tolerate. They murdered these Jesuit academics because they made the university an effective instrument in defence of the mass of the people, because they had become the critical conscience in a society of sin and the creative awareness of a future society that would be different, the utopia of God's kingdom for the poor. They were killed for trying to create a truly Christian university. They were killed because they believed in the God of the poor and tried to produce this faith through the university.

4

Who killed them?

Who killed them? This question always arises when there are notorious murders. Archbishop Rivera has stated that there is a strong presumption that it was the armed forces or the death squads related to them. The report by the Archdiocesan Legal Aid Office (*Tutela Legal*) on 28th November concludes after 38 pages of analysis that 'All the evidence, taken together, establishes that those responsible for the murder of the six Jesuits priests and the two women domestic workers were elements belonging to the Armed Forces.' It is difficult to explain, in fact, how in an area which was totally controlled and guarded by soldiers — who had already searched the house two days before and asked which Jesuits lived there — at 2.30 in the morning, in a state of siege and martial law, a large number of persons, about 30, could freely enter the house, remain there for a long time, murder eight people and destroy part of the building's installations, using lights, making a lot of noise and causing a visible fire, without being interrupted by soldiers in the immediate vicinity, and leave afterwards unchallenged. Furthermore witnesses present have testified that they saw these 30 men dressed in military uniform. Indeed — ironically and tragically — the Jesuits stayed in the house to sleep — despite their fear, reasonable in the light of their experience, that a bomb might be planted — precisely because the area was surrounded by many soldiers and they felt it was unthinkable that in these circumstances anyone would dare to make a physical attack on the house because it would be obvious who was responsible.

But what I want to stress here is not so much who actually did the killing, but who the real murderers are, those who promote the anti-kingdom and do not want God's kingdom of justice, fellowship, peace, truth and dignity to become a reality in El Salvador. It is a whole world of sin which has once more inflicted death on innocent people, people who worked for the poor. When they asked Archbishop Rivera who committed the murders, his reply was very straight: 'It was those who murdered Archbishop Romero and who are not satisfied with seventy thousand dead.'

This is the deepest and most challenging truth. It was the idols, the powers of this world, those who do not want anything important really to change in the country, even though they are forced to accept small cosmetic changes because the situation has forced them to. These murders prove that the idols are continuing to commit hideously barbaric acts and get away with them completely. It shows that there may have been a few changes in the country in recent years, but these changes come to a stop when they touch the idols. They tolerate elections, and in seven years there have been five elections, two for President and three for the Assembly. They tolerate a few reform laws, which are gradually watered down, they tolerate pressures from the US to control the death squads, they tolerate the millions of dollars that the US has given to improve the administration of justice — that is, so that it can begin to function at all — they tolerate that the huge military and economic aid be made conditional, so they say, upon their improving human rights.... But it has all been in vain. The idols continue active and recalcitrant, committing ever more wicked crimes. Therefore we need to understand well who really put these Jesuits and so many thousands of others to death. We must not confuse the physical authors of this horrendous deed with the actively idolatrous reality in El Salvador. These Jesuits, like Archbishop Romero, have forgiven those who actually did the deed because 'they know not what they do'. But they never forgave the idols, but lived and fought to destroy them.

I stress this point for several important reasons. The first and fundamental one is that real responsibility for these murders does not lie with the 30 men dressed in military uniforms who perpetrated the crime and destroyed part of the Archbishop Romero Centre. There is an 'analogy' in responsibility, and even though this is well known, we may recall it here. Of course those who thought up and carried out the crime are responsible. But many others are also responsible, to a greater or lesser extent, through their actions or omissions. Those who produce repression in El Salvador so that justice does not come to the country, share

30

the responsibility for the crime. In the US countless people today rightly accuse their own government of favouring a policy that is incapable of stopping the repression. But it is not enough just to say these things. What about all the governments in Europe and the rest of the world, claiming to be so democratic? What have they done effectively to stop the barbarous things that have been going on in El Salvador for the last fifteen years? What effective words have been uttered by religious leaders, episcopal conferences, universities in democratic and Christian countries? What have the Western media done during these years, when day after day human beings are dying of poverty and repression? Through action and above all through omission, many human beings have ignored, hushed up or distorted the tragedy of El Salvador. I can understand that for citizens of the first world it may be difficult to grasp the depth of this tragedy, because for those who take life and liberty for granted it is difficult to understand what poverty and repression mean in third world countries. Therefore they tend to ignore, fail to understand, and keep quiet. But perhaps they also keep quiet through an unconscious feeling of guilt. It is not possible to keep on living in abundance, having practically everything and wanting more and more, when many millions of human beings are dying of hunger every day. This whole set of actions and omissions is what causes the death of the poor and those who defend them. Therefore the question who murdered them is a question addressed to us all.

I am very aware and grateful from my heart that many people, communities and groups throughout the world have shown solidarity with El Salvador, and among them are priests, nuns, some bishops, some journalists, politicians and academics, many human rights institutions and many Christian or just honest men and women, who have given the best of themselves, their talents, their time, their possessions, even their lives for the poor of El Salvador. Now once more many of them have been expelled or forced to leave the country. As a symbol of all these people, I should like to recall the four North American women missionaries who gave their lives in 1980, the United States' most precious gift to El Salvador. They have the eternal gratitude of the Salvadorean people. But for the others, those who are not interested in the poor of this world, but only think about their own interests, 'national interests' — as rulers say — or simply want 'a better standard of living', without being horrified at the increasing abyss between the rich and poor countries, the causal relationship that

31

exists between the superabundance of some and the dire poverty of others, the freedom of some and the repression of others, for them these murders are a challenge, a call for conversion. For Christians, it is the inescapable demand required to place ourselves before this crucifix composed of the crucified peoples and ask ourselves what we have done and what we are going to do for Christ.

A second reflection is that these murders of priests and Jesuits occurred in the democratic and Christian Western world, as it likes to call itself, which invokes God. Indeed it says it invokes the true God and thereby defends him from marxists and atheists. We should not forget that Latin America, a Western and Christian continent, is the continent where there have been the most Christian martyrs since Vatican II. More than a thousand bishops, priests and nuns have been threatened in one way or another, imprisoned, expelled, tortured and murdered. And tens of thousands of Christians have been murdered for preaching the true word of God, for possessing a bible or the Medellin documents and putting them into practice. Given this, we cannot fail to ask ourselves what the Western Christian world's reaction would have been if these things had happened in Hungary or Poland, what an outcry there would have been in the US Congress or the British Parliament, what might have been said in bishops' conferences and in the Vatican. But the reactions of the 'official' Western world have been very slight compared to the size of the tragedy. It is because it refuses to recognise that the world cannot simply be split into good and bad people, Christians and democrats on the one hand and communists and atheists on the other. It refuses to recognise that the dividing line in humanity is idolatry, which is present everywhere, among so called communists and so-called democrats, so-called unbelievers and so-called believers.

At the very least the murder of these six Jesuits must make the Western Christian world honestly ask itself whether it is as good and holy as it says it is, whether it is as human and free as it claims. The murder should strip off the mantle of hypocrisy with which it tries to envelop democracy and freedom for the few at the expense of repression and poverty for many. It should lead to the suspicion at least that wealth, national security, individual freedom for the few necessarily generates idols who produce many victims in other places, even though these may be thousands of miles away. The murdered Jesuits insisted on this until the end of their days, and I remember that a very short time ago we were remarking with

32

Ellacuría on the absolute truth of the simple scriptural words: 'The desire for money is the root of all evil'. All those who seek to accumulate wealth and only think about living better and better should look at themselves in the mirror of the victims of this world and see plainly the evils they are causing.

Thirdly I want to reflect on the investigation that is demanded when notorious murders take place. It is natural that those close to the victims should demand one and understandable that, in some cases, those for whom the political cost of these murders is very high should also demand an investigation, the government of El Salvador and the US, in this case. But we need to be clear about what demanding and pursuing an exhaustive investigation means in El Salvador. There have been 70,000 murders and the only ones that have been solved — even then superficially and not in depth — are those of the four North American women and perhaps one other person. The case of Rutilio Grande, in spite of the promises of the President of the day, Molina, still has not been solved. The case of the five leaders of the Democratic Revolutionary Front (FDR), who were hauled out of the Jesuit school and killed in broad daylight, still has not been solved. The case of Archbishop Romero, although it has been investigated so much, is still notoriously unsolved. And if this happens in famous cases, it is easy to imagine what happens when unknown peasants are murdered, thousands of them, sometime in great massacres, as in El Mozote and Sumpul.... And this despite the fact that many human rights institutions have given important leads on the culprits. Various human rights organisations in El Salvador do this. Among them, with admirable objectivity are the Archdiocesan Legal Aid Office (Tutela Legal) and the UCA Institute of Human Rights. International institutions also provide information, Amnesty International in London, America's Watch in New York, CODEHUCA in San José, Costa Rica. For several years the UN special envoy, Pastor Ridruejo, has also been doing so, and in his October 1989 report he noted a worsening of human rights and an increase in torture in El Salvador. In special cases, when the murder victims are foreigners, as in the case of the murder of the Swiss Jurg Weiss and the French doctor Madeleine, there have been thorough investigations by representatives from the victims' own countries, which have given more than sufficient information to find the culprits. Nevertheless, in spite of all this information, with so many important clues and leads, the administration of justice in El Salvador has done very little serious investigating

33

indeed. Moreover, when the first government junta in 1979 appointed a special investigatory commission, it resigned as a body a few weeks later, when the second military junta of military and Christian Democrats came to power, because as a commission they were unable to do anything serious and they had a well-founded suspicion that those responsible for the crimes would never be brought to justice. Certainly some members of the commission had to leave the country. And on other occasions lawyers or judges conducting important cases were also threatened and had to abandon them.

So what is the point of the investigation which has been announced into the murder of the Jesuits? Hitherto investigations have achieved very little. Let us hope that this case will be investigated and the other 70,000 too, of course. Let us also hope that those who are now promising an investigation in order to convey a sense of normality and democracy first investigate why there have not been and could not have been any serious investigations in El Salvador. And let us hope they investigate why the vast majority of victims of notorious crimes — and also of course of the less well-known victims — happen to be people devoted to defending the poor.

Personally I have begun to be fed up with the very word 'investigation'. In our community when successive governments announced that they were conducting 'an exhaustive investigation' into a notorious crime, we used to comment ironically that a simple, normal, ordinary investigation would do because the 'exhaustive' investigations never come to an end. Let us hope that promises of investigation do not become an elegant excuse not to stop the repression. And let us hope the investigation of this case, if it is carried through to the end and those responsible are brought to justice, does not become a cover-up to distract people's attention from the 70,000 cases also needing investigation and does not become that most bitter of ironies, an excuse for saying that things are getting better in El Salvador.

The word 'investigation' has gone the way of other noble words like 'democracy' and 'elections'. They say little or nothing and are often used for the opposite of what they mean. Personally I sometimes think it is better that there should not be an investigation, and that it goes down in history that the murderer of Archbishop Romero and thousands of Christians was the sin of the world, the anti-kingdom, the idols. Because it is much more important to repeat and proclaim this great truth than to find out one day the name of the actual killer. And it is important not to let the idols and those who support them ease their consciences because, after all now it is known who pulled the trigger.

My fourth reflection is obvious. If it was possible to kill these well-known and respected Jesuits with impunity, some of them with international reputations, even when it was easy to foresee the world reaction that is now taking place, the high political cost, international pressures, if none of this could hinder the barbarity of murdering six priests, it is not difficult to imagine what defence peasants hidden away in little villages and country districts might have. Practically none. Even though it is obvious, it needs repeating. Who in the world is really working to stop this happening and demand an investigation of the El Mozote and Sumpul massacres, or the most recent one, on 31st October 1989 when ten trade unionists were murdered in broad daylight? This time the names of the two ordinary women who were killed are known, Julia Elba and Celina; their deaths are being investigated together with the Jesuits'. But countless others remain anonymous and their deaths are not investigated. As the Lord Jesus said, if they do these things with green wood, what will they do with dry wood?

My last reflection is something that has often come to my mind in thinking about Archbishop Romero. Of course it is important for the country to solve his case if this shows a desire for the truth and acts as some check on future possible murders. But I often have the feeling that investigating his case, and now that of the Jesuits, is like walking round corpses without any interest at all in what these murder victims were in their lives or bequeathed to us. The El Salvador and US governments are talking now about investigating the case of the six Jesuits. Let us hope they do it. But isn't it much more important for the country to remember what they did in their lives and to keep their spirit present?

The poor of El Salvador weep for their dead but what they want above all is that what they gave their lives for should remain alive. Isn't it more important to keep these martyrs alive than to investigate their corpses? Isn't it much more important for the country to hold on to the truth, mercy, justice and dignity for which they lived than to discover the names of their murderers? The latter is not at all easy, as we know, but the former is much more difficult and more necessary. Let us hope — dream — that one day the Salvadorean government, the US government and Congress will act on what these martyrs were in their lives,

35

seriously study the solution they proposed for the country, recognise the truth as they analysed it, acknowledge that without justice and without respect for human rights there can be no solution — with or without elections. These martyrs do not seek revenge, they are not even concerned with obtaining justice for themselves. What they want is that peace and justice should come to El Salvador and that in order for this to happen we should follow the best ways they showed us.

These are the reflections that come to my mind in connection with the murder of my six brother Jesuits. It is important to know who killed them, but more important to know why it was possible to murder them with such impunity, before, during and after the event. It is important to investigate the murders of the past, but much more important once and for all to stop murders happening in the future. It is important to solve notorious murders but more important to clear up the mass murder of peasants who die anonymously. It is important that justice should be done to my brother Jesuits in death, but it is much more important to keep them present by trying to keep alive what they were and did during their lives.

5

A new idea of a Christian university

These dark and tragic murders reveal some very important things. There are idols in this world and they produce victims, there is sin and it produces death. But when as well as murder it is martyrdom — there have been thousands in El Salvador — it testifies to what is the most important thing in our lives. With death we tell the truth about our lives and by their death these Jesuits told the truth about what they were and did. And because they died a martyr's death this also confirms that what they were and did was true. So now although it may seem a digression, I should like to mention three important things their martyrdom throws light on. What is a Christian university? What is the Church of the poor and liberation theology? These subjects are important, topical and disputed. They need illuminating and here these Jesuits bequeathed us an important legacy.

What kind of university did they leave us? Above all, they left us a new idea of a Christian university for our time, comparable in importance to that of John Henry Newman a century ago — and also many practical examples of the work of this new Christian university. When I was speaking about why they were killed I said a little about what the UCA meant to them. Ideally, of course, but also in many of its actual doings. In a word, what they left us was the belief that academic and Christian knowledge must be and can be at the service of the poor.

They wrote a great deal about this idea of a new Christian university in the service of the poor . And although in this book I have avoided long quotations, allow me — for the sake of brevity — one exception, a quotation from Ignacio Ellacuría's speech when he received an honorary doctorate from Santa Clara University, California, in 1982.

The starting point of our conception of what a University should be consists of two considerations. The first and most obvious is that the University has to do with culture, knowledge, a particular exercise of intellectual reason. The second consideration, which is not so obvious and commonplace, is that the University is a social reality and a social force, historically marked by what the society is like in which it lives. As a social force it should enlighten and transform that reality in which it lives and for which it should live...

Our intellectual analysis finds that our historical reality, the reality of El Salvador, the reality of the third world, that is, the reality of most of this world, the most universal historical reality, is fundamentally characterised by the effective predominance of falsehood over truth, injustice over justice, oppression over freedom, poverty over abundance, in sum, of evil over good...

This is the reality with which we live and have to cope and we ask ourselves what to do about it in a University way. We answer, firstly, from an ethical standpoint: we must transform it, do all we can to ensure that good predominates over evil, freedom over oppression, justice over injustice, truth over falsehood and love over hatred. If a University does not decide to make this commitment, we do not understand what validity it has as a University, much less as a Christian-inspired University...

A Christian-inspired University focuses all its academic activity according to what it means to make a Christian preferential option for the poor... The University should become incarnate among the poor, it should become science for those who have no science, the clear voice of those who have no voice, the intellectual support of those whose very reality makes them true and right and reasonable, even though this sometimes takes the form of having nothing, but who cannot call upon academic reasons to justify themselves.

Our University has modestly tried to adopt this difficult and conflictive course. It has obtained some results through its investigations, publications, denunciations; particularly through certain people who have abandoned other more brilliant, worldly and lucrative alternatives to devote themselves to making a University contribution to the liberation of the Salvadorean people; sometimes through students and staff who have paid very painfully with their own lives, exile, ostracism, for their dedication to the University's service of the oppressed majorities...

For this work we have been severely persecuted... If our University had suffered nothing during these years of passion and death for the Salvadorean people, it would mean it had not fulfilled its mission as a University, never mind displaying its Christian inspiration. In a world where falsehood, injustice and oppression reigns, a University that fights for truth, justice and freedom cannot fail to be persecuted.

There, in a few lucid words, is what these men thought about what a Christian university in the Third World should be. They arrived at this conclusion not just through theoretical reflection but also through historical experience of what a university in the Third World is. Therefore they were very much aware of the possibilities and also the danger of a university aimed at extending God's kingdom. Perhaps it sounds odd, but they were very aware that a university is also threatened by sinfulness, that it can serve the anti-kingdom, or more particularly, it can reinforce through the professionals it produces and through its social position the unjust structures in a society. Not only can a university do this but it frequently does, and introduces sin into society. Therefore these Jesuits were not at all naive about the possibilities of a university, but critical. They believed that, like any other human body, the university and its specific instrument, rational knowledge, is also threatened with sinfulness, and therefore that a Christian-inspired university must above all be a converted university. Conversion means putting all its social weight through its specific instrument, rational knowledge, at the service of the oppressed majorities. This is what these men wanted to do and did: in a university and Christian way they made an option for the poor.

So the final lesson remains — and perhaps it may be useful now when a document is being drawn up in the Vatican on Catholic universities — that a Christian university is possible in the Third World, a university that is not isolated in an ivory tower and stone-hearted towards the suffering of the poor, but a university sharing bodily in their suffering and hopes, a university with a heart of flesh. Another unforgettable lesson is that any Christian activity, including academic activity, is done in the presence of the anti-kingdom, which is opposed to it and fights against it. In the case of a university this may take the form of lies. The lesson remains that — as always happens, from the prophets onwards, from Jesus onwards, stating and analysing the truth means defending the poor and therefore confronting the oppressors. The lesson remains, the most important lesson that was these men's

39

life, that a university can be the voice of the poor, it can keep up their hope and help them on their way to liberation.

And we are left with the supreme lesson, that of the greatest love. Tragically, throughout history those who proclaim God's kingdom have to confront the anti-kingdom. It does not matter whether they do it as peasants, workers, nuns, priests, bishops, professionals or academics; they are all persecuted. These university Jesuits were also killed for defending the poor. And if the magnitude of the attack is in proportion to their defence of the poor, then we can say that the UCA's defence of the poor has been firm indeed.

6

Their Church

What kind of a Church did they leave us? It is a difficult and even polemical matter to speak of the Church today. The reader will understand that it is not at all my intention and neither is this the moment to enter into polemic or defend interests. It is a moment for sincerity before God and ourselves. Therefore in the presence of their corpses, I want to consider calmly the perennial and fundamental problem, raised again by Vatican II and Medellín, of what is the true Church of Jesus and what followers of Jesus, who are members of his body in history, should be like in our world today.

At the funeral mass in the presence of the six corpses, the papal nuncio called them true sons and members of the Church. And he gave them the name reserved by the Church for her finest children: martyrs. He is completely right, because they really were ecclesial. I have often said, sincerely and without irony, that although as is well known there have been many tensions between Jesuits and some members of the hierarchy, we Central American Jesuits have become more ecclesial in these recent years. The reason for this is that now we are more integrated within the people of God, we share more of their real life, we feel ourselves to be less elitist and triumphalist, more supported by the faith, hope and love of others, especially of the poor, the people of God. We are able to follow Christ better, and make him present in history, as we are his body making him present in the world as a sacrament of salvation. This is the Church given to us by Vatican II, to which we try to be faithful. Medellín stated very clearly that the poor offer the Church the greatest challenge. The Church cannot refuse to listen to them, it must live and die for their total liberation, in a word, the Church must be converted and become the Church of the poor. To that Church too we want to be faithful.

This is the Church the six Jesuits belonged to, which they also officially represented in their strictly priestly work. This, above all, is the Church they wanted to build. In this Church they lived and enjoyed themselves but also suffered. The Church hurt them when it did not measure up to circumstances, when it looked more to its own interest as an institution than to the suffering of the people, when some of its officials lacked understanding and were indifferent to the suffering of the people, rejecting their best aspirations, when — incomprehensibly — they silenced Archbishop Romero. On the whole the Jesuits thought the Church is turning in on itself, that little by little it has tried to silence Vatican II, Medellín, Archbishop Romero, the ecclesial base communities, religious life in Latin America. And how they suffered because of this! That is also why they were critical within the Church, of course in a free and mature way, and they thought that prophetic denunciation within the Church was a great and indispensable service to it, whereas adulation and servility — which are always rewarded — were grave wrongs done to the Church. In a word, they knew they belonged to the Church, they wanted the best for the Church and above all, they wanted and worked to build the best possible Church for the Salvadorean people.

If I recall these things, it is because their martyrdom helps us all to clarify and solve a serious Church problem, which is growing rather than diminishing. For some years now, particularly in Latin America, an old problem has resurfaced: what is the true Church? We are not talking about it now in dogmatic terms, of course, but in operational terms. It is not very clear by what actual name the true Church is officially called today. It tends to be along the lines of 'communion' effectively understood as submission from below upwards. Its 'mystery' is rightly stressed. But the term 'people of God' is discredited and suspect. This way of talking enables the Church to detach itself from the historically lowly, the poor. Thus it withdraws from seeking inspiration from the poor, from the spirit of the beatitudes, the light that shines from Yahweh's suffering servant. Although such a Church does some good to the poor, it does not make them central within it, or see service to them as its central mission.

On the other hand, in Latin America we have the expression 'Church of the poor', the Church that makes the poor of this world

42

central to its mission and shape. This Church of the poor is treated with suspicion when it is called the 'popular Church', meaning a dangerous and mistaken way to be a Church, in order to discredit or condemn it. We all know this and many suffer for it. We suffer because this Church is often condemned by those who do not know it and are unwilling to converse with it. Above all, we suffer because it is not recognised or gratefully accepted that this Church of the poor, with all its limitations and mistakes, is producing a great deal of faith, much hope, much love and much martyrdom.

I say all this now without bitterness and with the hope that these six new martyrs, together with so many others, may make us all reflect. These murdered Jesuits enjoyed the friendship and respect of some — very few — brother bishops. Certainly they were intimate friends and close collaborators with Archbishop Romero and they often collaborated fraternally with Archbishop Rivera. Bishops like Pedro Casaldáliga have been in our house and felt at home there. Catholic bishops and bishops from Protestant sister churches visited us in the UCA and we conversed in a friendly and Christian way as members of the people of God and the Church of Jesus, each with his own function and specific charisma. But in some way these Jesuits were also seen as members and representatives of a supposedly dangerous Church, one which was disobedient, suspect, perhaps even unorthodox. In their pastoral work as priests they were accepted in the archdiocese and some of them were invited, exceptionally, to give talks and retreats to other priests. But as a whole they were not very well regarded by many bishops in El Salvador and in Central America. Their ideas, their theology, their commitment were suspect. None of them, not Ignacio Ellacuría, nor Amando López nor Juan Ramón Moreno — to name the three who were professional theologians — were normally invited to offer their theological ideas, useful though they were for the country's grave problems and those of the Central American region as a whole. One Salvadorean bishop, now retired, publicly accused us UCA Jesuits of being the cause of all the evils, including the violence in the country. Through caution in some cases, through positive rejection or disagreement with them in others, these men who had much to offer the Church were ignored and sometimes even attacked from within. They came under suspicion of belonging to the 'popular Church' or of exercising a so-called 'parallel magisterium'.

Again, without any harshness or bitterness, I should like these martyrs, together with so many other Christians, to help us reflect on this burning Latin American issue: what is the true Church of Jesus? In order to decide we can and should use various criteria: communion with the hierarchy, orthodox formulation of the faith, and so on. But it would be dangerous and fundamentally absurd if other more fundamental and primary criteria were not also used to judge what the essence of the Church is. Doesn't the true Church exist when — as well as communion from below with the hierarchy — there is also communion from above with the people of God, the poor of this world, those really preferred by God? Doesn't the true Church exist where, as well as traditional sacramental and apostolic practices, there is a determined effort to preach the gospel to the poor, to communicate and put into practice God's good news for them, solidarity and commitment to them, to the point of sharing their cross? Doesn't the true Church exist when — as well as obedience and faithfulness to what has been handed down by tradition — people are obedient and faithful primarily to God's will for today, even to the point of giving their lives?

I have formulated all this as a rhetorical question because the answer is obvious. We do not have to choose between the things I have mentioned, but it is important to stress what has priority. To serve the Church and the hierarchical Church is important for a Christian and a Jesuit of course, and these men always did any work they were asked to do. But we should not forget something even more obvious and fundamental: that the Church is the sacrament of something greater than herself, a sacrament of the kingdom of God and the God of the kingdom. Our final loyalty cannot be to the Church, but in the Church to God and the poor, because God is greater than the Church. Telling the poor the good news is the reason why the Church exists at all, as Paul VI beautifully put it in his exhortation *Evangelii Nuntiandi.*

This produces tensions, as we all know, which we must endure honestly and fully with charity and hope. However that should not make us loose clarity. We truly love and serve the Church when, within it, we de-centre it in favour of the kingdom of God, when we make the Church a sacrament of something greater than itself, when it becomes a sign of God's kingdom and wholly devoted to the poor of this world, for whom the kingdom of God exists. This is what these Jesuits' life in the Church was about, and the lives of so many others. This, although many will not accept it, is their greatest contribution to the Church. This is what makes them awkward, of course, but their shake-up of the Church is not to destroy it, as some indeed claimed, or to weaken or attack it. On the contrary, it is to help it become more the Church of Jesus.

This Church, as I have said, is commonly called the Church of the poor, and pejoratively, the popular Church or parallel Church. I do not wish to deny that there are exaggerations or mistakes in this way of being the Church, sometimes an excessive politicisation or dependence on popular political movements. This occurs more in some of its leaders than among the ordinary Christians who make up the base communities. In fact, this problem has been discussed in some of the UCA's publications with criticism of what appeared to need criticising.

But this being said, even admitting the limitations and mistakes of the Church of the poor, there is something that cannot be ignored and it would be dangerous and wrong to do so, and for the institutional Church itself to do so. This Church of the poor is the most active and creative Church, it is the most involved in the people's just causes, it is the Church that does the most in the community to overcome the endemic evil of individualism, including religious individualism. It is the Church that arouses the most hope to overcome resignation, that does most to unite what is Salvadorean and what is Christian, and certainly the Church that generates the most mercy, justice, commitment and love for the suffering people. If we are seeking criteria and want to know how the Church behaves, we cannot ignore these realities. Another thing that cannot be ignored is that this Church has been ferociously persecuted, it has generously shed its blood and produced innumerable martyrs, who are the proof of the greatest love. And if the end of life is what expresses the deepest truth about life itself, it cannot be denied that in this way of being a Church there has been a lot that is Christian. If so many have died like Jesus, it is because so many lived like Jesus. This is what is illustrated in the life and death of Archbishop Romero, the murdered priests and nuns, so many ordinary Christians, catechists, preachers of the word, members of base communities, and now these six Jesuits.

It would be tragic for the building of the kingdom of God and the building of the real Church to take as a criterion of truth what is important but secondary and to spurn what is primary and essential. We all know this but need to remind ourselves. El Salvador and all Latin America have given proofs of incredible faith and incredible love. There are countless martyrs in our countries, and if this greatest love is not a criterion of what makes a true Church, we may well ask what is. Let us recall that not all members of the Church have been persecuted; many have been favoured and flattered by the oppressors. The ones most like Jesus were the ones who were persecuted, those who, like him, truly opted for the poor. And that is why the persecution takes no account of denominations: Catholics, Lutherans, Episcopalians, Baptists, Mennonites — all have suffered persecution when they served the poor.

Let us say in conclusion that these murdered Jesuits felt a deep affection for the Church. Isn't this the moment, in the presence of this new bloodshed, together with the blood of so many priests and nuns in Latin America, and above all in the presence of the blood shed by so many Christians in the communities in Latin America, to reaffirm the Church of the poor? It is urgent and necessary for the good of the poor and the Church itself, to point out once more with serenity, truth and justice the anomalous situation in which a Church that is more committed and producing so many martyrs is suspect, whereas the church groups with little commitment are not persecuted at all and not suspect at all either. It is urgent and necessary that there should be dialogue within the Church, a calm, friendly dialogue in which all are prepared honestly to admit their own failings, and in which all are open to the love of those who shed their blood. We owe it to them and on them we will be able to build a Church which is a true communion and a true Church of the poor.

7

Their theology

What theology did they leave us? Let us say a little about liberation theology too. Clearly this is not the moment for a petty and self-interested apologia, but a moment to reflect deeply on the truth of things and theology. Let us not forget that one of the murdered men, Ignacio Ellacuría, was a well-known theologian, and so too were Amando López and Juan Ramón Moreno. They all tried to do liberation theology. In order to grasp what light their martyrdom can throw on theology, let us recall the type of objections which are commonly made to it, again not in a polemical spirit but a spirit of calm reflection.

As is well known, this theology has long been criticised and, fortunately, the first to criticise it were the powerful of this world. With great perspicacity — from their point of view — it was severely criticised and attacked in influential US analyses, from the Rockefeller report to the two Santa Fe reports written by advisers of Reagan.* It was also criticised later by CELAM and the Vatican in its first Instruction, though it softened its critcism in its second Instruction.** All this is well known and I will not go into it here, because there have already been many replies, and

---

* Two papers produced by the 'Santa Fe Committee' of the right-wing US think-tank, the Council for Inter-American Security, purporting to analyse Communist subversion in Latin America through phenomena such as liberation theology. The first, 'A New Inter-American Policy for the Eighties' (1980), set out guidelines for the incoming Reagan administration, and was followed by a similar analysis in 1988: 'Santa Fe II: A Strategy for Latin America in the Nineties'.
** Congregation for the Doctrine of the Faith: *Instruction on Certain Aspects of the 'Theology of Liberation' (Libertatis Nuntius)*, 1984; *Instruction on Christian Freedom and Liberation (Libertatis Conscientia)*, 1986.

Ignacio Ellacuría wrote an excellent long article in response to the first Instruction.

I would rather discuss here other charges against liberation theology, some well-intentioned, some ill-informed, and some based on total misunderstanding, more a reaction of self-defence against the questions raised by this theology. I think that this is a good way to get to the essence of liberation theology.

Some say that liberation theology is not scientific enough, that of course it is inspired by faith but it is uncritical and even naive. Others, on the contrary, say that liberation theology is basically elitist, an academic pursuit that does not reach the great majority. Many say, or imply, that liberation theology has now given all it had to offer and has gone out of fashion. I think that there is some or much truth in these criticisms, depending on the particular case, but they do not reveal the whole truth or even the most important truth about liberation theology. Certainly, they do not reveal the truth of liberation theology as practised by these Jesuits.

The truth is that liberation theology must advance in all kinds of knowledge, in intellectual self-criticism and in its capacity for systematisation. Ignacio Ellacuría frequently stressed this, and he was a thinker of genius who could never be accused of undervaluing the intellectual component of theology. In fact in the UCA we sometimes asked theologians from other countries to help us with the immense capital of theological knowledge they possess, the libraries and time, all of which we lack here. And remember a poignant symbol: the theological library of the Archbishop Romero Centre was partially destroyed after the murders. We are very grateful to the theologians who have assisted us in all this, especially Jesuit and non-Jesuit theologians who have come from Spain to bring us things we lacked, including some of their positive and friendly criticisms and who also came — as they kept telling us — to learn to do theology in El Salvador.

Having said this we still need to ask which theology, among the academic and scientific varieties, has captured the essence of scripture and the gospel, of God's word for this moment of history, if we believe that God is still speaking today to his creatures. We still have to ask which theology has given a response to humanity's greatest current problem, which is the devastation of God's own creation through poverty, oppression and death. We need to ask which theology has made it its business to combine faith and justice, theory and practice, which theology has united theology and spirituality — in the option for the poor. We are fully aware of our limitations and any help or criticism is cordially welcome. But it would be impoverishing and mistaken for academic critics of liberation theology to ignore its novelty and strictly intellectual contribution, its capacity to rediscover absolutely fundamental things about God's revelation, which have slept the sleep of the just for centuries in academic and scientific theologies, its rethinking of the nature of theological knowledge, its reformulation of the concept of verification of theological truths, etc. Ignacio Ellacuría made an outstanding contribution to this work, insisting that theology should take seriously the signs of the times, so that theology should be the raising of social reality to the status of a theological concept, that theology should be understood as the theory of a historical and ecclesial praxis. (Personally I have reformulated this by saying that theology is *intellectus amoris, misericordiae, iustitiae.*)

There can be honest discussion about whether liberation theology covers many branches of the subject, and it can certainly be asked to systematise these branches better. But I am convinced that it offers us all fundamental knowledge about God and this world, which is really true, serious, reasoned and well argued, and if you like, scientific. In any case, at least for brother Jesuits who want to do theology, the theology of these Jesuits, liberation theology, shows that it is the most Ignatian theology in the world today, because it is guided by the search for God's will in order to put it into practice and by its following of Jesus today, the Jesus who was poor and lowly.

It is also true, as others say, that liberation theology, as a technically formulated theology, does not reach the majority of ordinary people, who generally do not even know the name of this theology or of any other. If you like, liberation theology is done by 'professionals'. But none of this means that it is elitist, pursued by members of an elite in their studies and read by others in their studies too.

Liberation theology is not — directly — a theology for the masses, for the people, any more than any other conventional theology is, but it is related very specifically to the lives of the mass of the people because it deals with their real situation, certainly their poverty, their suffering and hope. Not only that; it also draws on many of the reflections and popular theologies of the communities. Those who do theology about this situation may be few, an elite; but the situation they study is that of many, the poor. Ignacio Ellacuría kept on saying that theology might be done sitting in a study but its starting-point was not the study but the poor. The theological truth that is discovered from their viewpoint is returned to them, even though the forms in which it reaches them are not academic, obviously, but little leaflets, sermons, biblical reflections in the communities, song books etc. If the mass of ordinary people today understand a little better that what they are suffering is the sin of the world, that God is a God of the poor, their God, that what Jesus proclaimed was a kingdom of life and justice for them, that it was for this that he suffered the fate of the poor and was murdered; if these poor people feel a little more encouraged to work and struggle generously and nobly for life to belong to all, then, even if they have not heard a word of liberation theology, it has still reached them.

Lastly, it is true that liberation theology cannot rest on its laurels. It must address new problems, as it is trying to do: popular religion, the indigenous religions, women, ecology... But what takes my breath away is when people keep saying that liberation theology has gone out of fashion. Of course, it is possible or even probable that this or that book or writer on liberation theology may be going out of date, and as time goes by all of them may gradually become so. But none of this means that liberation theology as such is not — unfortunately — very topical and very urgent, in fact increasingly so. Dom Luciano Mendes de Almeida, the Brazilian Jesuit who is president of the Brazilian bishops' conference, once said, 'Liberation theology has put its finger in Latin America's wound.' This was true then and it is still true today. Oppression in the Third World is not a fashion, but something very present and increasing. Latin America's wound is not healing but growing bigger and more infected. As Ellacuría repeatedly said, God's creation has not turned out that well and it is getting worse. Today there are more millions of poor people in the world than yesterday and fewer than there will be tomorrow.

So it is very important to remember and hold on to the fundamental point: liberation is correlative to oppression and oppression and injustice are still with us and increasing. Poverty is increasing in the Third World, the gap between the rich and poor countries is widening, there are wars — more than a hundred since the last world war and all of them in the Third World. Cultures are being lost through the imposition of foreign commercial cultures... Oppression is not a fashion. The cries of the oppressed keep rising to heaven and, as Puebla says, more and more loudly. God today goes on hearing these cries, condemning oppression and strengthening liberation. Anyone who does not grasp this has not understood a word of liberation theology. What I ask myself is what theology is going to do if it ignores this fundamental fact of God's creation as it is. How can a theology call itself 'Christian' if it bypasses the crucifixion of whole peoples and their need for resurrection, even though its books have been talking about crucifixion and resurrection for twenty centuries? Therefore if those doing liberation theology are not doing it well, let others do it and do it better. But someone must keep on doing it. And for the love of God, let's not call it a fashion.

Let us hope that the day will come when oppression, demeaning and unjust poverty, cruel and massive repression cease to exist. On that day liberation theology will be obsolete, and this is the day that liberation theologians are working for, even though on that day they will be out of a job. But while oppression lasts — and all the statistics show that Latin America is getting poorer — liberation theology is necessary and urgent. It is the only theology that defends the poor of this world — or at least the only one that does so seriously. And let us remember that it is a theology that has martyrs like Ignatius of Antioch and Justin in the early centuries, which, as always, shows that at least it has been a Christian theology.

I do not want what I have been saying to sound abrasive, much less a defence of personal interests, which have little place in my thoughts at the moment. But I do want this to be an appeal for seriousness in theology. The corpses of the Jesuits show that this theology is not elitist but of the people, because it has risen in defence of the people and shared the people's destiny. They show that this theology has said something serious, even scientifically and academically. For let us not forget that what was most feared in these men was their serious and reasoned word, their theological word. They show that oppression — taking the form here of brutal murder — goes on being a horrific reality to which theology must respond. If it does not, it is in vain that it calls itself Christian.

8

Their legacy

So what remains? After these reflections, digressions almost, I'd like to return, in conclusion, to the fact of the murder itself and ask myself what remains in Salvadorean history and deep in the hearts of us who are still alive. I said at the beginning that for me this murder and martyrdom has been different from all the many others. On other occasions, at the funeral masses of martyrs, together with the sorrow there was a feeling of hope and even pride and joy in being Christian. This time things have been different and the question what remains has been forced on me in a different form. In this case my answer is very personal, but I hope it will go beyond the personal and say something for everyone.

Above all the suffering people remain and they have lost some of their protectors. These murders happened in a week of war which left about a thousand dead, countless wounded, many poor houses destroyed and poor people forced to leave their homes and seek refuge elsewhere, as has happened so many times in El Salvador. Others will have the task of political and ethical analysis of the responsibility for what happened, the rightness or wrongness of the FMLN action in the city during these days. And they will have to analyse and judge the reaction of the armed forces. But as always, what is clear is that a people remains who during this week have been even more impoverished, terrorised, and whose hopes of peace have been dissipated yet again.

This is the context in which I see the ultimate malice of the murder of these Jesuits. They have murdered men who defended the poor and the poor are even more unprotected. And if to these murders is added the persecution campaign during these days against all the churches — something Bishop Rosa Chávez explicitly condemned — the meaning is very clear: the people are now more helpless. During these days Catholic priests have been murdered, churches full of people seeking refuge have been attacked, Archbishop Rivera and Bishop Rosa Chávez have been threatened and the Salvadorean government even asked John Paul II to remove them from the country. Many members of the Lutheran Church, the Episcopalian Church, and of the Baptist and Mennonite communities, have been attacked and captured. Many priests, other Christians and social workers were threatened with death, in earnest. Bishop Medardo Gómez of the Lutheran Church had to leave the country under diplomatic protection. And of course they have tried to intimidate and muzzle the UCA, the Christian university.

There has been, in other words, an attempt to dismantle the Church of the poor, to take from the poor the support and defence these churches offered. Salvadoreans know all too well what this means. During the years 1977-80 they tried to dismantle the Church in the first big wave of persecution, and we all know what an irreparable loss was suffered in the murder of Archbishop Romero, priests, nuns, catechists, members of base communities... Little by little they have been recovering and now again they are trying to dismantle the Church and its defence of the poor. This is the nub of the question and the ultimate malice of these murders: the Church is left decimated and the poor even more unprotected. The murder of the six Jesuits has been first and foremost a great loss for the poor. And as has been said before, before the Church made an option for the poor, the poor had already made an option for the Church, seeking support and hope in her that they could not find anywhere else.

The pain, the doubt, the darkness remain too, and we must not trivialise it. We should not be surprised or ashamed if during these days we feel Job's desolation at God's silence and Jesus' cry on the cross: 'My God, my God, why have you forsaken me?' It is not easy to find light and courage in this situation of repression and death, in which the poor are ever more impoverished and weakened. At least for me it has not been easy this time to say from the beginning the true and scandalous words we said on other occasions: 'Martyrs are the seed of life'; 'Let us give thanks to God for our martyrs'. I do not deny the truth of these words, but I did not find it possible to utter them at once and certainly not as a matter of course.

So what really remains from the martyrdom of these six Jesuits? I believe and hope their spirit remains, that they rise again, like Archbishop Romero, in the Salvadorean people, that they continue to be a light in this dark tunnel and hope in this country of endless misfortunes. All martyrs rise again in history, each in their own way. Archbishop Romero's is exceptional and unrepeatable, but Rutilio Grande is also present in many peasants, the North American women are still alive in Chalatenango and La Libertad, Octavio Ortiz in El Despertar, and the hundreds of martyred peasants in their communities.

The martyred Jesuits too will live on in the Salvadorean people. Fr Lolo will live on the Fe y Alegría schools and among the poor who loved him so much for many years. I do not know how the UCA martyrs will rise again. I would like it if the Salvadorean people remembered them as witnesses to the truth, so that they go on believing that the truth is possible in their country; that they remember them as witnesses to justice — structural justice, to put it coldly, or more expressively, love for the people — so that the Salvadorean people retain the courage to believe that it is possible to change the country. I hope they remember them as faithful witnesses to the God of life, so that Salvadoreans go on seeing God as God their defender; that they remember them as Jesuits who tried to undergo a difficult conversion and paid the price for defending faith and justice. This is what I hope these Jesuits leave the Salvadorean people and that in this legacy they go on being alive, an inspiration and encouragement.

I should like the Church and believers to remember them as those witnesses to the faith spoken of in the Letter to the Hebrews, and above all, as followers of the great witness, Jesus, whose life is summed up in Hebrews as compassion for the weak and faithfulness to God. Translated into Jesuit language, may they be remembered as men of justice — the present-day version of mercy — and as men of faith in the God of life in the presence of death — the present-day version of faithfulness. I hope my brothers will stay alive in this legacy.

I hope too that when peace and justice comes to the country, succeeding generations remember that these Jesuits were among those who made it possible. I hope that future Christian generations remember their contribution to creating a Salvadorean faith and Church, that they are grateful for their witness to the fact that faith and life in El Salvador are not contradictory but empower each other. I hope they recognise that in this way these martyrs guaranteed that faith in Jesus was handed on in El Salvador. I hope, then, that in future Salvadorean Christians will be grateful to them that the country has attained justice and grown in faith.

The price to be paid for all this has been very high, but inevitable. Today, when we hear so much about evangelising cultures, we should remember a deeper form of evangelisation: the evangelisation of social life, so that society itself becomes good news. And for this to happen it is necessary to become incarnate in that reality, as Archbishop Romero said in words that make us shiver to this day: 'I am glad, brothers and sisters, that they have murdered priests in this country, because it would be very sad if in a country where they are murdering the people so horrifically there were no priests among the victims. It is a sign that the Church has become truly incarnate in the problems of the people.'

These words, so brutal at first sight, are far-seeing. There can be neither faith nor gospel without incarnation. And with a crucified people there can be no incarnation without the cross. Ignacio Ellacuría said many times that the specifically Christian task is to fight to eradicate sin by bearing its burden. This sin brings death, but taking it on gives credibility. By sharing in the cross of the Salvadoreans the Church becomes Salvadorean and thus credible. And although in the short term this murder is a great loss, in the long term it is a great gain: we are building a Church that is really Christian and really Salvadorean. Christians have shown truly that they are Salvadoreans and thus that Salvadoreans can really be Christians. This is no small fruit of so much bloodshed in El Salvador, Salvadorean and Christian blood: that faith and justice should walk hand in hand forever.

Finally they leave us a cry to the whole world that does not want to listen, that easily ignores the cries of anonymous peasants but this cry at least it cannot ignore. This cry is an accusation and a call to conversion. 'Blood is the most eloquent of words,' said Archbishop Romero. World reactions — even though I do not know whether they will be strong enough to stop the tragedy — have made many people think. I am told that even in the US Congress tough men wept.

They also leave us good news, a gospel. On this sinful and senseless earth it is possible to live like human beings and like Christians. We can share in that current of history that Paul calls life in the Spirit and life in love, in that current of honesty, hope and commitment that is always being threatened with suffocation but that time and again bursts forth from the depths like a true miracle of God. Joining this current of history, which is that of the poor, has its price, but it encourages us to go on living, working and believing, it offers meaning and salvation. This is what I believe these new martyrs leave us. With it we can go on walking through history, humbly, as the prophet Micah says, in the midst of suffering and darkness, but with God.

In El Salvador today there is much more darkness than light and the question of hope cannot be answered as a matter of course. In one of the letters I received from El Salvador a great Christian woman wrote to me:

> Suddenly it seems that everything has been like a dream and I see all our martyrs going about their daily business. I am not worried about the fathers because I know that they are enjoying our heavenly Father with their robes washed in the blood of martyrdom, but I think about their families and all of us who are still here.

It is not easy to know how to keep on hoping and we must all answer this question in our own way. It seems that everything is against hope, but for me at least, where I see there has been great love, I see hope being born again. This is not a rational conclusion and perhaps not even theological. It is simply true: love produces hope and great love produces great hope. From Jesus of Nazareth, with many before him and many after him, whenever there has been true love, history has gone on, people have been forgiven and offered a future which hopefully they will accept. Many human beings and Christians have been given that hope. And together with the great love these martyrs had, there are the faces of the poor, in which God himself is hidden but nevertheless present, asking us to keep going, a request we cannot ignore. The history of sin and grace continues, the history of the poor goes on and the history of God. To keep going in the midst of such darkness is not at all easy, but it is something the poor and the martyrs help us to do so that it becomes possible. It is something we owe the poor and these martyrs.

My six brother Jesuits are at rest now in the Archbishop Romero chapel under a big picture of him . All of them and many others will have given each other a warm embrace and been filled with joy. Our fervent desire is that the heavenly Father send this peace and joy very soon to all the Salvadorean people. I have written these pages essentially in the hope that the memory of these new martyrs may contribute to peace, justice, dialogue and reconciliation among all Salvadoreans.

Rest in peace Ignacio Ellacuría, Segundo Montes, Ignacio Martín-Baró, Amando López, Juan Ramón Moreno, Joaquín López y López, members of the Society of Jesus, companions of Jesus. Rest in peace Elba and Celina, beloved daughters of God.

May their peace give hope to us who are still alive and their memory not let us rest in peace.

29 November 1989